Between Still Water & Shore

A Collections of Reflections in Poems

By

Michael Gonzalez

Library of Congress Control Number: 2026907520

Printed in the **United States of America**

For information or permissions contact:

Michael Gonzalez

Dedication

To the ocean and the rain. To the ocean, which does not ask to be understood, yet carries everything that has ever been surrendered to it. To the rain, which falls without preference, touches the broken and the whole alike, and does not linger to witness what it heals. You are the two great metaphors this book was written inside of. Patient. Relentless. Indifferent in the tenderest way. This collection is for every soul who has stood at the edge of something vast and found, in that vastness, not an answer, but the courage to keep standing. And for those who have felt the rain and called it grief, only to realize, much later, it was simply the world washing you clean.

Contents

About the Author

Michael Gonzalez is a poet, thinker, and lifelong student of the human condition, forged in the streets of the South Bronx and shaped by the rhythms of New York City. Raised in the Tremont neighborhood of the Bronx, his early years were defined by the raw textures of city life, the corner of Delancey, the pulse of Harlem, the quiet endurance of communities that outlast every storm thrown at them. A graduate of Northeastern University with a Bachelor of Science degree, Michael pursued his studies with a focus in Mathematics and a minor in Business, disciplines that trained him to see the world in patterns, systems, and underlying truths. That same analytical precision runs quietly beneath his poetry, giving his verse a structural depth that belies its lyrical surface. His life has taken him across multiple cities and occupations, from New York to Florida, each transition adding new layers to a voice that was always listening, always documenting. He has worked across industries, worn many identities, and carried within each of them the sensibility of a writer who sees not just what is, but what the moment is trying to say. Influenced by the legacy of the Harlem Renaissance and the street-level lyricism of artists such as Nas and William Kris, Michael writes in the tradition of poets who refuse to separate beauty from truth, or the personal from the universal. His work moves between the upbeat and the contemplative, between the block and the cosmos, between the self and the city it was built inside of. This collection is his most personal work to date: an exploration of impermanence, identity, survival, and the grace found in motion. It is the voice of a man who has lived in many places and carries all of them with him, still writing, still witnessing, still finding poetry in the space between where he has been and where he is going.

Page Blank Intentionally

A Brief Echo

The day unfolds without intent,
a wandering breeze, a sky half-bent.
It neither warns nor makes amends;
It simply moves, begins, then ends.

The gods stay distant, cold, and still,
their silence deeper than my will.
I walk beneath their vacant throne,
a traveler learning the art of solitude.

What comes will come — the dusk, the flame,
the joy that stutters through my name,
the grief that settles like a stone.
I greet them both as if unknown.

No hour is mine to hold or keep;
time drifts softly like ghost-born sheep.
I breathe, I stand, I fade, I fall —
a brief echo against the wall.

And when the night unthreads my form,
I'll bow to its indifferent storm —
a spark that flickered, soft and slight,
then folded back into the endless night.

Michael Gonzalez

Beneath Indifferent Stars

The gods keep their silence,
And silence is the only law.
We walk beneath it,
like shadows stitched to the earth,
pretending our steps matter.

The river does not care
If I drown or drink.
Its current is a sermon
spoken in a tongue
that mocks my need for meaning.

I light no candles.
I bow to no altar.
The stars are indifferent
hanging above me,
And I bleed only because I am alive.

So let me be brief:
I am a passing wind,
a cracked hymn in the throat of time.
If joy comes, I will not chase it.
If sorrow comes, I will not resist.
Both are masks worn by the same face.

Signal in the Static

The voice comes through like a trembling wire,
half static hiss, half gospel fire.
It rises, falls, then splits in two,
a signal searching for what's still true.

Some nights the air is a wounded drum,
beating out names that never come.
Some nights the sky is a busted speaker,
The world grows louder, the heart grows weaker.

I talk to myself in the radio's glow,
a ghost on the dial only I can know.
Memory crackles in broken bars,
a choir of shadows, a map of scars.

The past keeps calling collect at night,
asking if I've learned how to hold it right.
But I'm just a man with a borrowed tune,
a voice that flickers like a dying moon.

Still I speak — because speaking's a flare,
a spark thrown upward to anyone there.
And maybe the world, in its static roar,
hears something worth tuning toward once more.

So I send my breath through the trembling air,
a fragile hymn, a stubborn prayer —
hoping the signal, thin and bare,
finds someone listening
somewhere.

Michael Gonzalez

Nothing Stays

Nothing stays.
Not the wind that names my skin,
not the hour that pretends to hold me,
not the quiet voice inside
that keeps trying to sound like the truth.

The world moves without asking.
It lifts its shoulders,
shrugs off my longing,
let the day fall open
like a book written for no one.

I walk through it anyway —
a brief pulse in the throat of time,
a flicker learning how to vanish
without begging for a witness.

Let the gods keep their distance.
Let fate do what it always does:
arrive uninvited,
leave without apology.

I will meet each moment
as if it were a stranger
I owe nothing to,
yet still greet
with a bowed head
and an unguarded heart.

A gentle Bike Night

Three hours rolling under moonlit skies,
Tires whisper softly where the darkness lies.
Streetlamps flicker like a guiding line,
Turning the neighborhood into something divine.

Cool night air brushing past my face,
Every corner holds its own quiet grace.
The world feels wider when the roads are bare,
Just me and the night in a gentle affair.

Pedals turning steady, heartbeat slow,
Time drifting by in a silver glow.
Three hours riding with nothing to chase—
Only the hush of the night and the open space

Michael Gonzalez

A River Impermanence

Look long enough at a river
And it stops being water.
It becomes a theory of motion,
a lesson in how nothing
ever holds the shape you give it.

The surface glitters like certainty,
But certainty is just sunlight
pretending to stay still.
Beneath it, the current
rewrites itself endlessly,
a body that refuses
to be the same body twice.

I tell myself I'm observing —
as if observation were neutral,
as if the river doesn't change
because I'm looking.
But everything alters under attention.
Even the self.
Especially the self.

Maybe that's the point:
to watch something
that cannot be held
and admit you're the same.
A moving thing
trying to understand motion.
A mind trying to map
What it's made of.

Between Still Water & Shore

The river keeps going,
unbothered by my questions.
It doesn't care
whether I understand it.
It only asks that I witness
the way it dissolves
and reforms
and dissolves again —
a reminder that existence
is just a series of brief agreements
between what is
and what was.

Michael Gonzalez

A River Rhyme

Look long at a river and watch it slip,
a silver thought on a trembling lip.
It keeps no promise, holds no form,
a quiet rebellion against the norm.

The surface glitters like truth made thin,
a mirror pretending to stay within.
But underneath, the currents revise.
Every story they memorize.

I stare as if looking could make it stay,
as if vision weren't washing away.
But everything shifts beneath the gaze —
The self, the world, the passing days.

Maybe the river is teaching me.
How fragile a thing identity can be:
a moving line, a borrowed shape,
a door that opens only to escape.

Still it flows, unbothered, free,
unconcerned with philosophy.
It asks for nothing but to be seen,
to shimmer briefly, then leave clean.

And I, who try to hold it fast,
learn that nothing is meant to last —
That looking is only a fleeting truce
between what I witness
and what I lose.

After life

I slipped beyond the silver veil,
Where silence hums, where stars exhale.

The body I knew dissolved like rain,
Yet still my spirit bore its name.

Awakened now in a stranger's skin,
A borrowed frame, a life within.

Their heartbeat drums, yet mine it sings,
Two histories bound by hidden strings.

I walk their streets, I speak their tongue,
Yet echoes whisper where I'm from.

A child's laugh, a lover's cry,
Ghostly shadows passing by.

The afterlife is not an end,
But doorways bent, a path that bends.

We trade our masks, we shift our guise,
And learn to see through others' eyes.

So when you meet me, do not fear,
I've lived before, I still am here.

In every soul, in every flame,
We rise, we fall, yet stay the same.

Michael Gonzalez

Again

Morning hits hard, even when it's soft,
light sliding in like it owns the place.
You move through the motions anyway,
same cup, same breath, same door —
But something in the air feels older than you.

The street looks normal until it doesn't,
until the shadows lean a little strange,
until the wind carries a hint of something
You can't name but feel in your ribs.

Routines turn gritty when you look too close —
like you're walking the same path
in two different worlds at once.
One is the life you know.
The other is the one watching you back.

And in that thin space between steps,
The spirit slips through —
not gentle, not grand,
just real enough to shake you awake.

Angel's Help

Angels whisper softly when the night feels cold,
Lifting up the spirit when the world feels old.

Guiding every heartbeat through the shadows you roam,
Turning every lonely road into a path back home.

A breath you didn't know you needed, a push on heavy
days.
Angels don't descend in flashes; they show up in small
ways—

The spirit isn't distant; it's the strength you carry inside,
The voice that keeps you moving when the world feels hard
to ride.

Michael Gonzalez

April 2

April hums in a trembling key,
a message caught between sky and sea.
The wind pulls the clouds once worn,
a half-made song on a shifting shore.

Some days the light is a cracked-blue shell,
spilling a truth too soft to tell.
Some days the rain is a whispered dare,
a voice that rises from thinning air.

I walk through the month like a broken chord,
a man out of tune with his own reward.
Memory sparks like a faulty fuse,
flaring at moments I didn't choose.

The past keeps calling in static tones,
asking if I've paid off all my loans —
not money, but promises, thin as breath,
owed to the ghosts I left for death.

Still I listen — because listening is grace,
a way to stay tethered to time and place.
And maybe April, in its fragile spin,
Let's a little more mercy in.

So I breathe with the wind, let the signal flare,
a stubborn hymn rising thin in the air —
Hoping the month, with its trembling light,
keeps me tuned
to what feels right.

April

April speaks in a trembling pitch,
a frequency caught between wound and stitch.
The air is a wire the wind plucks thin,
a song that forgets where it should begin.

Some days the sky is a cracked-blue shell,
leaking a light too soft to tell.
Some days the clouds are a choir of ghosts,
humming the names I miss the most.

I walk through the month like a half-tuned chord,
a man out of sync with his own reward.
Memory flickers like a faulty fuse,
sparking at moments I didn't choose.

The past keeps calling in a static hum,
asking if I know where I came from.
But April answers with a shifting breeze,
a truth that bends like broken knees.

Still I listen — because listening's a prayer,
a way to stay tethered to thinning air.
And maybe the world, in its quiet spin,
Let a little more light seep in.

So I breathe with the wind, let the signal flare,
a fragile hymn rising thin in the air —
Hoping the month, with its trembling grace,
Let's me stay present
in this place.

Michael Gonzalez

Behind The Viel

I trust the before more than the shine,
the mess unposed, behind the crooked line.
The future pulls like a hunter's snare,
a bloody lure swinging in the air.

Time drags forward, a stubborn beast,
hauling scraps from its endless feast.
I chase the bait, though I know the trick —
The moment I reach it, it vanishes quickly.

Did I call the future a dangling prize,
a red-meat promise before my eyes?
Maybe I'm strung on an unseen thread,
led by a hand I've never read.

Because when I get there, it's never there —
Just now again, the same thin air.
Refresh, refresh, the cycle hums,
And every "after" becomes what comes.

Behind me, before me, stack high and tight,
a tower of ghosts in fading light.
And still the world insists I climb,
Though every step feels the same in time.

Broken Dreams

The luxurious gate, a promise bright,
Reflects the harsh and fading light.
The hopeful steps, a steady drum,
To reach a place they've dreamed to come.
They carry bags of fragile things,
Of futures built on paper wings,
And stories told of streets of gold,
A legacy for young and old.

The concrete cracks, the neon burns,
A lesson that the spirit learns.
For here the soil is dry and thin,
Where winners rise, and dreams begin,
But many fall and find their space,
In the shadows of this promised place.
The work is hard, the pay is low,
The seeds of hope refuse to grow.

The accents fade, the tongues grow tied,
As different selves are cast aside.
The hands that built, now serve and clean,
A ghost of what they might have been.
The mirror shows a stranger's face,
Lost in this unforgiving space.
A silent grief, a heavy toll,
For fractured heart and broken soul.

The anthem plays, the banners wave,
Above the hopes they could not save.

Michael Gonzalez

And still the stories are retold,
Of fortunes brave, of heroes bold,
But in the quiet of the night,
They count the cost of faded light.
A freedom bought, a dream in pawn,
Beneath a cold and distant dawn.

Ezekiel

When the hours stretch thin
and the sky feels unwilling to change,
when every dream you carried
seems to fade at the edges—
There is still a whisper rising.
This force will bring renewal.

Not all long nights are endings.
Some are the breath before dawn,
the quiet where roots deepen
and unseen things take shape, like the wind.

For there comes a moment
when the delay breaks open,
when the horizon brightens
not with what was lost,
But with what is finally ready.

The days are at hand—
not distant, not forgotten—
and visions once dimmed
lift their heads up high again.

Hope does not vanish;
It waits.
And when it steps forward,
It steps in fullness, by the grace of God
Allowing you to keep on living.

Michael Gonzalez

Failure to exist

The world arrives before I do.
By the time I notice the light,
it has already changed its mind.
Reality is a rumor
my senses keep trying to verify.

A mountain stands —
But only because my eyes
haven't looked away yet.
Turn once,
and the whole thing collapses
into unobserved dust.

Thought is slower still.
It chases the moment
like a scholar chasing a comet,
cataloging the tail
long after the fire is gone.
Every idea is a post-mortem.

To exist is to lag behind.
To be a witness
to what has already slipped
into the archive of the unrepeatable.

And what am I,
If not, the sum of these delays —
a consciousness arriving late
to its own life,
a shadow trying to catch
the body that casts it.

Maybe failure is the point.
Maybe existence is nothing
But the attempt to name
What refuses to be held.
A gesture toward meaning
in a universe that keeps
politely declining.

Still, I reach —
because reaching is the only proof
I have never been here at all.

Michael Gonzalez

Free Spirit 1

In silent depths, where shadows sleep,
A vast, uncharted ocean deep,
The subconscious holds its tide,
Where fears and hidden memories reside.

It hums a tune, a quiet plea,
For harmony and clarity.
A tangled web of what has been,
The inner world we live within.

Then comes the call, a gentle sigh,
From ancient winds that sweep the sky.
The Third Domain, the Spirit's grace,
Descends to find its proper place.

It is no storm, no lightning flash,
But morning light on dewy ash.
A current calm, a holy stream,
That wakes the soul from a troubled dream.

It sifts the sands, it parts the sea,
Of tangled thought and history.
It clears the fog, it stills the waves,
The grace the inner being craves.

The tuning begins, a subtle art,
A whispered word to mind and heart.
The Spirit breathes, the waters clear,
Dispelling doubt and calming fear.

Between Still Water & Shore

The mind aligns, the body knows,
The unseen garden where it grows.
For in this blend, this sacred tune,
The human and divine commune.

Michael Gonzalez

Good Trouble

You run your thumb along the fracture,
that small break in the surface
Everyone else pretends not to see.
But you know it's there —
a chip that didn't ruin you,
Just marked you.

People talk like perfection is the point,
Like a clean edge means a clean life.
But you've lived enough days
to know the truth hides in the damage,
in the places where the world
pressed too hard
And you didn't shatter.

A chip is a story,
a record of impact,
a quiet testament
that something tried to break you
and failed.

So you carry it —
not as shame,
But as proof.
A flaw that glints in the right light,
a reminder that even the cracked things
can hold more than they were built for.

House of Pain

They say God lives in steeples,
but you've seen Him in stranger rooms —
in cracked sidewalks, in dust-heavy air,
in the quiet corners where no one looks twice.

Holiness isn't polished;
It shows up rough,
like a whisper dragged through gravel,
like truth that refuses to dress itself up.

You've felt the sacred in places
That don't make the postcards —
a dim hallway, a back porch,
a night when grief sat beside you
and didn't speak, just stayed.

If God has a house,
It's built from breath and bone,
from the moments that break you
And the ones that stitch you back.
No stained glass — just raw light
finding its way through whatever cracks you carry

Michael Gonzalez

A Letter to Young Poet

Your colors speak louder than any praise I could give,
Shaping whole worlds in the space where your shadows
live.

You pull light from the quiet, strength from the dark,
Each stroke a reminder that vision is its own kind of spark.

I see the fight in your lines, the calm in your hand,
a story carried farther than most people understand.

Keep painting your truth, let the canvas unfold —
Your work is a fire the world can't hold.

Lost on Shore

Rhyme

The sea keeps secrets under its skin,
Pulls at the light till it's paper-thin.
It lays the day on the stones to dry,
a half-made prayer beneath the sky.

I walk the shore where the wind grows wild,
salt in my throat like a grieving child.
The gulls keep laughing their jagged tune,
mocking the heart that breaks too soon.

Every wave is a rumor of what I lost,
a name I buried, a line I crossed.
The tide rolls in with a ghost's cold hand,
asking what pieces I still command.

Salthill remembers what I forget —
the vows I whispered, the quiet regret.
It holds my shadows in shifting foam,
gives every sorrow a place to roam.

Still, I stand where the water bites,
ankles numb in the fading light,
waiting for something I can't reclaim,
a face, a moment, a whispered name.

And the sea keeps singing its ancient song:
Leaving is easy; returning is wrong.
Yet here I linger, stubborn and still,
drowning again on the edge of Salthill.

Michael Gonzalez

Lost on Shore

The sea keeps its own counsel.
It drags the light out thin,
lays it across the stones
Like a blessing, it forgot to finish.

I walk the length of the shore
pretending the wind knows my name,
pretending the gulls aren't laughing
at how small a person becomes
When memory pulls harder than gravity.

Every wave is a rumor
Of something lost —
a face I can't recall clearly,
a promise I never meant to keep,
a version of myself
I left somewhere in the tidepool years.

Salthill is a place that remembers
even when I don't.
It holds the ghosts gently,
Let's them shimmer in the shallows,
let's them vanish when the sun shifts
just a little.

I stand there anyway,
ankles cold,
Heart brined and stubborn,
waiting for the sea to tell me
What I already know:

That leaving is easy,
but returning
is its own kind of drowning.

Michael Gonzalez

Mass Appeal

Voices gather like storm clouds,
low at first, then rising bold.
A hundred hearts beating in time,
lifting what one alone can't hold.

Sound swells like a tide returning,
pulling every soul into its sway.
Grief, joy, memory — all of it carried
in a single wave of praise.

No one leads; the moment leads.
No one shines; the whole thing glows.
A choir made of breath and struggle,
of every story no one knows.

And when the final note breaks open,
The silence feels like something earned —
a room washed clean by voices
that rose, collided, and returned.

No Heavy Load

The day arrives without asking,
soft as a breath you didn't notice leaving.

Nothing demands your name,
Nothing insists you stay.

The world keeps moving
with or without your witness.

You walk through the hours
like a guest in your own life,
touching the furniture of existence
without claiming any of it.

Even joy feels borrowed,
a brief warmth in the palm
before the wind takes it.

Still, there's a strange comfort
in this looseness —
a freedom in not belonging,
in letting the world be the world
and yourself be a passing shadow
that harms nothing.

Call it resignation,
call it clarity,
call it the quiet truth
that everything dissolves
and that's its own kind of grace.

Michael Gonzalez

Ode 1

Start with a name
that tastes like a drum,
a name that walks into the room
before you do.

Praise it sideways.
Praise it slant.
Praise it like you're polishing a mirror
that refuses to show your face.

Let the line break
where the breath breaks,
where the truth stumbles,
where the joke lands crooked
But still lands.

Say the world is a bruise
you keep pressing
to see if it still hurts.
Say the world is a hymn
you only half-remember
But still hum anyway.

Invoke the ancestors —
not the ones in portraits,
But the ones who haunt
Your syntax,
Your swagger,
Your shadow.

Let the ode be a door
that opens inward and outward
at the same time.
Let it be a trick.
Let it be a dare.
Let it be a confession
You disguise as a boast.

And when you reach the end,
don't end.
Pivot.
Swerve.
Turn the whole poem
back on itself
like a snake biting its own tail,
like a question that refuses
to stay answered.

That's the secret:
An ode is never finished.
It just keeps singing
long after you stop writing.

Michael Gonzalez

Ode 2

Start with a name that thunders low,
a drum in the chest where the echoes go.
Praise it crooked, praise it sly,
Praise it like a truth that refuses to lie.

Let the line break where the breath missteps,
where the heart stutters, where the rhythm wept.
Let the joke land sharp as a blade,
a grin in the dark that the shadows made.

Say the world is a bruise you press,
a hymn half-sung in a tattered dress.
Say the world is a door unlatched,
a spark in the night that can't be matched.

Call on the ghosts who taught your tongue,
The elders hummed when you were young.
Let them swagger through every line,
Their fingerprints smudged across your spine.

An ode should twist like a serpent's kiss,
a loop of meaning you almost miss.
It should boast, confess, and then deny,
a truth that laughs as it passes by.

And when you think the poem is through,
swerve — let it turn and look at you.
Because an ode won't end;
It circles back like a long-lost friend.

Prisoners Dilemma

I speak in sentences sharp as wire,
each one lit with a quiet fire.
They rise from places I never name,
soft with sorrow, stiff with no blame.

The world keeps asking me to bend,
to smooth my edges, make amends.
But every truth I try to say
breaks loose and stumbles its own way.

My thoughts are fugitives on the run,
chased by the echo of what I've done.
Still, I gather them, line by line,
hoping one might sound like mine.

If language saves me, let it be
a cracked-open hymn of honesty —
a sentence trembling in the air,
half confession, half repair.

Michael Gonzalez

Prisoners of Time

A quiet hum, a constant drone,
For every seed of effort sown.

The morning greets a weary face,
A daily, hurried, breathless race.

To climb the rungs of gilded stairs,
Ignoring pleas and silent prayers.

The ledger fills, the profit swells,
A hollow sound, like ringing bells.

That toll for dreams put on the shelf,
To serve a master, not yourself.

But then the clock's decisive chime,
Releases prisoners of time.

A breath of air, a hopeful sigh,
Beneath the vast and open sky.

The screen recedes, the world returns,
A lesson that the spirit learns:

That work's a means to find the key,
To unlock joy and truly be.

For passions found in simple things,
The laughter that a good book brings.

The taste of food, a whispered word,
A song of life, so long unheard.

Between Still Water & Shore

So one life toils, a driven soul,
To reach a distant, final goal.

The other finds its truest art,
In tending to a restless heart.

A fragile peace, a subtle shift,
Between the grind and every gift.

Michael Gonzalez

Ritual

Morning slips in like a quiet spell,
light folding itself across the room
as if it's been here before
in another life, another name.

Every motion feels older than you —
the cup lifted, the breath taken,
The door opened to the same street
that somehow shifts beneath your feet.

Patterns turn to portals
when the mind goes still enough.
A simple step becomes a crossing,
a small task becomes a sign.

In the hush between moments,
Something unseen stirs —
a reminder that even the plainest days
carry a pulse of the divine.

See as Free

You try to walk a straight line,
but the world keeps bending —
corners softening, edges drifting,
language loosening in your hands.

Every rule you learned
starts to feel like a fence
built for someone else.
Your voice wants out,
wants wild,
wants the kind of shape
that refuses to stay still.

You speak, and the words scatter,
choosing their own gravity.
You breathe, and the rhythm breaks
in all the right places.

Call it free verse,
call it rebellion,
call it the moment the spirit
Finally stops asking permission.

Some truths don't fit the form —
So you make a new one,
built from breath,
from instinct,
from the raw pulse
of whatever refuses
to be contained.

Michael Gonzalez

Silence

It's easy for them to say
Your life must be smooth,
as if you were a map
that guarantees the terrain.
As if your appearance were a key
that unlocks every locked door
without splintering the frame.

But you know better.
You know the body carries
its own weather system —
storms no one else sees,
fault lines no one else feels.
People look at you
and think they've read the whole book
from the cover alone.

They don't see the nights
You folded yourself small,
the years you learned silence
like a second language,
The way grief taught you
to walk without echo.

They want the shorthand version —
the easy story,
the clean narrative arc.
But you are not a symbol.
You are a constellation
of bruised stars and stubborn light,
a history written in margins
They never bothered to read.

And maybe that's the truth.
You carry like a hidden pain:
No one's life is easy
when they're busy surviving
the story of someone else
Keeps trying to write for them.

Michael Gonzalez

The Path

You stand at the edge, where the future takes hold,
A canvas unpainted, a story untold.

The shadows may whisper of what used to be,
But a new dawn awaits, wild and wonderfully free.

Don't let yesterday's burdens weigh down your flight,
For within you, a power burns, radiant and bright.

Each step that you take, though faltering or grand,
Is a brushstroke of courage across life's vast land.

The mountains may rise, and the rivers may flow,
Challenges beckon to help you grow.

Embrace every struggle, each stumble and fall,
For lessons are learned, standing bravely and tall.

So breathe in the hope, let your spirit ignite,
Chase dreams with a passion and shines ever bright.

The path may be winding, unknown, and obscure,
But the strength that's within you will always endure.

To Exist or Not to Exist

The world appears in fragments first,
a shimmer, a glitch, a half-made burst.
By the time I name it, it's already gone,
a ghost of a ghost I mislooked upon.

Light hits the wall, then slips away,
a vision too slow to make it stay.
I chase the moment, but it resists,
Teaching me gently how nothing exists.

The mountain stands, but only seems—
a borrowed shape inside my dreams.
The mind arrives a second late,
Missing the door it meant to create.

Still I reach—a stubborn act,
Trying to hold what won't stay intact.
The world dissolves, but leaves a trace,
a shadow learning to keep its place.

And I, who fail at being real,
Am just a pulse I sometimes feel?
A flicker caught between breath and dust,
Trying to exist because I must.

Michael Gonzalez

Unburdened Existence

The world moves without urgency,
a slow turning of light and shadow
that asks nothing from you.
You stand inside it like a visitor,
unburdened by purpose,
unclaimed by desire.

What comes, comes.
What leaves, leaves.
The day unfolds with the same indifference
as a tide that neither loves nor hates the shore.

You learn to meet it gently —
to let the hours pass through you
like wind through an open window,
touching nothing they don't need to.

There is a strange grace in this:
to want nothing,
to resist nothing,
to simply be a quiet witness
to the brief miracle of existing.
a small light opening itself
just enough for you to walk through.

Call it wisdom,
call it surrender,
Call it the soft truth
that life asks only to be lived,
not mastered.

Ways of Life

Morning comes the same way every day,
soft light slipping through the blinds,
coffee warming the hands that still remember
what they've held and what they've lost.

The world moves in small circles —
steps to the door, breath in the air,
the same street, the same sky,
Yet something shifts each time.

There's comfort in the pattern,
a rhythm the body knows by heart,
a quiet promise that even the simplest acts
Can keep a life stitched together.

And in those repeated motions,
Something tender rises —
proof that even in the ordinary,
The spirit finds a way to speak

Michael Gonzalez

Whatever You Need

You say you're fine, but the air around you
trembles like a wire pulled too tight.
I see the weight you're hiding,
the way your breath stutters
before you let it go.

If you need silence,
I'll sit with you in it.
If you need fire,
I'll strike the match.
If you need a place to fall apart,
I'll hold the pieces
without asking where they came from.

Some people offer help like charity —
clean, distant, safe.
But I know better.
Need is messy.
Need is holy.
Need is the place where the spirit
Finally tells the truth.

So whatever you're carrying,
whatever shape your hurt takes today,
I'll meet it.
Not to fix you —
but to stand beside you
while you remember
you were never meant
to carry it alone.

Who Am I?

My name is a seed in a foreign land,
carried in pockets, cupped in a hand.
It whispers stories I barely know,
roots that tug where I cannot go.

My mother spoke magic under her breath,
words that could bargain with life or death.
I learned them crooked, half-asleep,
syllables buried somewhere deep.

The world says choose — be this or that,
shed your skin like a worn-out hat.
But I am the river between two shores,
a door that opens to other doors.

abracadabra, open — the old refrain,
a chant that rises like monsoon rain.
I speak it softly, throat gone tight,
hoping the past will spark to light.

I walk with ghosts who share my face,
names I carry from place to place.
Their shadows hum in my blood's slow drum,
calling me back to where I'm from.

And still I wander, half-in, half-out,
a man of longing, a man of doubt —
Yet every word I claim as mine
Turns the lock to hinge, and spine to spine.

Michael Gonzalez

46

THE END